Out-patients

Elisabeth Murawski

SERVING HOUSE BOOKS

Out-patients

Copyright © 2010 Elisabeth Murawski

All rights reserved.

No part of this book may be used or reproduced in any manner whatsoever without the prior written permission of the copyright holder except for brief quotations in critical articles or reviews.

Cover art: Wilhelm Lehmbruck, "Seated Youth," Andrew W. Mellon Fund, Image © 2010 Board of Trustees, National Gallery of Art, Washington, 1917, composite tinted plaster, 1.032 x .762 x 1.155 (40 5/8 x 30 x 45)

Author photo: Charles Gannon

ISBN: 978-0-9825462-8-4

Serving House Books logo by Barry Lereng Wilmont

Published by Serving House Books

www.servinghousebooks.com

First Edition 2010

*For my brother John Murawski (1931-1998)
and his wife, Marie Murawski (1936-2004)*

Acknowledgments

These poems first appeared in the following journals:

Alembic	Rome, Starry Night
Attic, The	The Injury
Bellevue Literary Review	Aneurysm
Blackbird	The Black Madonna
Blue Mesa Review	Memories of Logan Square
Caprice	The Kiss
Commonweal	Reaching Darien
Comstock Review	Fever
Crab Creek Review	The Other Son; Prescription
Folio	The Visit
Fulcrum	Serbian
Illuminations	Prize
The Journal	towards five
North American Review	To a Daughter-in-Law
pacific REVIEW	Migrant
Poet Lore	Wake of Brother Ray
Poetry Northwest	Driving on Empty; Out-patients
Southern California Review	Abu Ghraib Suggests the Isenheim Altarpiece
Southern Humanities Review	Quicker than the Eye
Tar River Poetry	For Rosemary
TIFERET: A Journal of Spiritual Literature	This Morning in Winter

"Widower" first appeared in the poetry and fiction collection *Free Parking* from The Spirit That Moves Us Press.

Note: "Abu Ghraib Suggests the Isenheim Altarpiece" won the 2006 Ann Stanford Poetry Prize.

I would call these dry-eyed, uncompromising poems dark, but they are shot through with light: the lay-everything-bare fluorescent light of hospitals, the cold clarity of winter mornings, the revealing flash of photography. (This collection contains the only successful poem I have seen thus far to come out of the onslaught of images from the Iraq War, "Abu Ghraib Suggests the Isenheim Altarpiece.") While never flinching or turning away from the unsightly decrepitude of our mortality, Murawski with her poet's eye can also transform an aging mother scrubbing a Corningware coffee pot into a sun-flooded masterpiece by Vermeer. Among the out-patients here—the sufferers and caregivers, the dead and their survivors—we meet prodigal sons, snake handlers, "a Palestinian St. Joan," widowers and would-be suicides, and Keats himself, slowly drowning of tuberculosis in a room in Rome whose gilded ceiling is carved with daisies. Murawski works in a hard-won, spare and nimble free verse, but also writes a mean sonnet (as in the Keats-answering "Reaching Darien"). Against the frailty of the body, she posits the stubborn strength of the spirit: "We push back death / like a cowlick / hoping it will hold / for the time being."

—A.E. Stallings

Contents

9	Aneurysm
10	towards five
12	Driving on Empty
15	Fever
17	Migrant
18	On a Sunday
20	The Injury
21	Memories of Logan Square
23	The Kiss
24	The Other Son
25	This Morning in Winter
26	Prize
27	Quicker than the Eye
28	Abu Ghraib Suggests the Isenheim Altarpiece
30	The Prescription
32	Rome, Starry Night
34	Reaching Darien
35	The Visit
37	Wake of Brother Ray
38	Widower
39	The Black Madonna
41	For Rosemary
42	Serbian
43	To a Daughter-in-Law
44	Out-patients

Aneurysm

She is two inches above the ground,
mind cleared by a fist.

The German word for clear is *hell*.
The machine her breath:
up and down breasts,
up and down death.

No more
wrong sides of the bed.

The transparent
skin of a soul
wears out.

Her mouth is full of sky.

towards five

towards five
the time the light
turns magical
so that even New Jersey
looks beautiful

towards five
the time a bullfighter
dies in Lorca's
litany
a las cinquo de la tarde

my first grandchild
barely more than
a seed will
slip from this life
sucked like dirt

from a rug
the procedure clever
as a phoney shower
sterile as a hospital
birth   this life

slated to be brief
as a poem
will leave us
at five o'clock in the afternoon
we in the stands

will join hands
as if in a church
to witness this
tenacious matador
with squatter's rights

step out
onto the sand
without cape or sword
to face the stunning
bull's eye

Driving on Empty

She's lifted her face,
reduced her bust, tried
hypnosis to lose

her passion for country
breakfasts and double fudge.
She's compared herself

to the child-women
he likes to fix cars for—
skinny waitresses from Waldorf

in smirking eye-shadow.
Knows what they look like—
stole the film once

from his Instamatic. He took
pictures on the boat.
She continues to compare

herself until her cells
whirl off-kilter, three-
quarters of her stomach

slips under the knife.
The oncologist hunts
the nodes.

It's after chemo,
when she is not quite
ready for a hospice,

she sees Jack make a pass
at the visiting nurse,
slip a fifty in her purse.

A psychic told her once:
"You will live to be
ninety

and find a second husband
who truly loves you."
One day he asks her to sign

two blank checks
"just in case."
She rallies, enraged,

but it doesn't last.
Morphine drips
through the hole in her chest.

She is too weak to protest,
or doesn't care,
he is there for her last breath.

Unable to face her dead,
or her friends,
he squelches plans for a service.

He takes the ashes home
and places the urn
on the mantle

under the mirror he uses
to fix his tie,
smooth his stubborn cowlick.

It's not as much fun
fooling around,
now she's gone.

He's never liked to be alone.
Between sex and Valium
it's hard to choose.

Just outside the window
is her feeder for the birds.
He takes to sitting where

she used to sit for hours,
sometimes with tears
he's at a loss to explain.

Fever

It is intestinal, your wife says malaria
and calls in wizards and astrologers.
But you know it is Spain, Vallejo,
burning you up town by town.
You know it is the Indians
back home in Peru, the streets
running red, glazing over your eyes,
shaking your teeth in your head
like boxcars.

The precious or dreadful moment
stood on its head for you
to predict the end.
Your pain was always possible.
Your pain never had a cause.
Any more than these irises,
this joy in guitars,
the love affair with dolmens
under blue sky,
under parallel pines.

You will cry out on Good Friday
"I am going to Spain!
I want to go to Spain!"
So much returning.

You must ring the bells
in the cathedrals.
You must kiss the children
and walk with them in the parks
pointing out the spirits in the stones.

They will X-ray you, the doctors,
and find nothing wrong.
Tell them to X-ray
the stones. Close your fingers
on the stones that bring you peace.

Speak to the stones
as you spoke to the little ones
learning to read your life.

Your wings are not broken.
You live in these woods.
Solar.
Ultimate.

Migrant

Sometimes at night in his sleep
Alfonso will cry out
because he has lost her again.
His goddess
who speaks to him in his own language.
Who dries his tears
when he mourns the deaths of young children.

It is she who shows him the sun
when he sweats in the lettuce fields,
teaches him to breathe it in
with each nostril
so that the sun swells inside him
and kicks against his belly
like an unborn child.

It is her hand touching his hand
laid against a mirror,
her fire burning the soles of his feet
when he climbs the rock
above the platinum river, calm as ice.
She tells him: your father's toenails
must be like claws now
in the grave. You cannot break
the chain of sea and sand.

Shivering, he listens to her sing
the perfect note
he can never remember hearing
before it breaks his heart.

On a Sunday

A Palestinian St. Joan
praised by Hussein, her name's
called out like a prayer
from the minarets.

She was not religious,
a friend says; *she didn't
pray or cover up.* What
possessed Wafa Idris,

a Red Crescent worker
who raised doves
and adored children?
Dropping fingers in a bag?

An arm? Holding the mortally
wounded young?
She does it
two days after the boy

Samir dies, fifteen.
The blast, shattering
windows on Haffa Road,
decapitates her,

kills an Israeli
grandfather, injures
scores. With laptops
and cell phones, the press

invades the family home.
Her mother shrieks
anathemas. Chicks
scatter underfoot. A serene

Wafa, fixed forever
in cap and gown,
looks on from a frame.
A few reporters who linger

hear the bitter wail:
I have lost my daughter!
and then the sobs, the cooing
laughter of the doves.

The Injury

Eyes patched with gauze
my son in his hospital bed
tells me how his father
gave him St. Paul to read
on fornication. *See
what your mother is doing.*

A nurse pokes her head
through the door,
asks, *sotto voce*, how
we are. Beyond habit,
I don't answer
from our pitiful nighttown.

My sin. My son.
Nothing's working. Clenched
in his second wind,
I cut the visit short.
Leaving, I feel
his white patches follow me.

In the car, therapeutic,
I roar with the windows up.
Soon, he calls to badger.
No more of you, he mutters.
The phone's asleep in its cradle.
The silence is thrilling.

Memories of Logan Square

It was just a drill,
not German bombs.
A low flying plane
dropping sandbags
on Diversey Avenue.

Two blocks from home
we waited in the dark
for the all clear,

seeding nightmares
of Nazi soldiers
breaking down doors
to find me,
anywhere,

their helmets
black and shiny
as water beetles.

Two years. Three.
Russia had the bomb.
I stopped talking to trees.
I prayed rosaries
to Our Lady of Fatima,
obsessed about melting
dummies in newsreels,
the war in Pyongyang.

It took decades
to discover why
I cried for your daughter's
first steps. It wasn't,
as I thought then,
the threat of death
by shock
or aftershock, the fungus
blossoming
on Chicago sky.
It was knowing again

my life pulled up short
by the orange tip
of a cigarette
weaving through the dark.
The breaking in
like a shoe.
The slow death of concubines.

The Kiss

Waking before dawn, he reached
and found an empty space. Careful
of the boy and girl asleep,

he searched and searched the house,
feeling his legs wilt
nearing the garage.

And there she was, tilted
on the Nissan seat, hair splayed
out like Goldilocks'.

It was chilly that night
without a note. Was her gown
drifting off

one he'd never liked?
Maybe, later, he'll tell
someone close

what he did in disbelief,
as if only he
could bring her back to life:

the shake, the slap, the kiss.

The Other Son

My father welcomes the prodigal.
He would hoist him to his shoulders
if he could.

As for me,
who can be trusted,
I know I speak with half a mouth:

pity my brother's bloodshot sorrow,
his sores
that will make him blind.

I stay here in my tent
brooding on the equity of rainfall.
The fig leaf bursts into life.

There is this scent of carnation.

This Morning in Winter

I climb from sleep
with nothing to lose.
Outside, the marble trees

shine. The sky's so
ordinary it's strange.
I study for age the skin

in the crook of my elbow,
lie here, stripped
of veneer, awaiting

with empty hands
the absurd bridegroom.
Oh to be trusting as a tree

in the status quo, robbed
of leaves yet supple
in the wind below zero.

Prize

She looks at me
through a caul of forgetfulness.
Does she want to be

understood? She who
could not watch
her own mother die

but locked herself in
the bathroom,
vomiting. I ask myself

why should I?
She was like
the morning glory's trumpet

in late afternoon,
disappointingly
folded in on itself,

hiding her heart
from view. I stroke
her hand, its skin

thin as a petal, knowing
she will never play
the music I hoped for.

Quicker than the Eye

In a stiff towel
the dying cat raises its paw
to the knot in the tree.

The wild child screams,
fastens his fist
on the wall,
at once one
with the crushed lung,
the jagged ribs reaching down
into a past idiom.

Like magnified thrustings
of bulbs coming up
through the world's weight,
the warm belly
writhes
then grows still.

The moon,
turning back the night
as if it were the tide,
lies caught in fire.

Abu Ghraib Suggests the Isenheim Altarpiece

Arms behind him shackled to the wall,
Jamadi's knees buckle. He lands on air.
Let us reposition him to stand erectly,

homo sapiens, place the irons higher up
on the window bars. When again he falls
forward, hangs like Jesus from his wrists,

call it faking, possum-playing. Persist.
Lift him up on legs that ragdoll-sag
into a third collapse, the effect

grotesque as Grunewald's Christ: bones
about to pop from their sockets. The silence
curious, raise the hood that hid a face,

asphyxiation, wag a finger past the eyes.
It has begun, the turning of the skin
to purple, the indigo of Tyre and Sidon. Note

as he's lowered to the floor, the stunning
rush of blood from nose and mouth,
the Red Sea. In this heat, let us blur

the time of death, pack the flesh in ice
like fish or meat, pretend he's merely
sick, hooked to an I.V., a patient

on a stretcher. Destroy the crime scene.
Throw away the bloodied hood. It stings
with the quality of mercy.

Note: This poem is based on material in "A Deadly Interrogation" by Jane Mayer, *The New Yorker*, Nov. 14, 2005.

The Prescription

What she needs is to be arrested
for something she did not do,
for being who she is.

Give her a cell,
damp and dark with bugs,
no windows, inadequate

toilet facilities.
Provide sadistic guards,
the threat

or more than a threat
of torture.
No paper or pencil.

If she were to be thus
deprived,
if you confiscated

her jewelry,
if you burned every book
in her library,

and if once and for all
you separated her
from her children,

she might right herself
like an overturned beetle,
and having reached

Gethsemane on all fours
she might finally learn to die
and what it means to die.

Rome, Starry Night

It's late. Tomorrow,
Vatican City, the tomb
of St. Peter

crucified upside down.
Windows without screens
let in mosquitoes,

the horns of Fiats.
Sipping bottled water,
I trust one special photo

will turn out—the ceiling
Keats died under
even as he got his wish

to be among the English
poets, daisy after daisy
ornately carved

and gilded, each flower
framed on a field of blue
by strips of white.

At dinner tonight, my son
asked for a sign,
a proof when I die

there is an afterlife.
Just tap me here. He grabbed
his shoulder. My airy

sure was writ in water.
What ceiling will be mine?
I close the shutters

on this city of last things,
undress in the dark.
I think of the trout circling

in the window tank. A waiter
snatched it with a net.
Solemn in its turning

overhead, the ancient fan
clicks and spins,
a wheel of fortune.

Reaching Darien

In Rome the cradle city forced to die,
lover, friends a world away asleep,
your need for magic fevers while you keep
watch, flicker of the tongue a speech, a lie
to calm the green Severn, his painter's eye
possessing you for history. The deep
lungs' wrench he's never seen, the final heap
of fossil yet unpressed, the crooked sigh.
You promise with a surgeon's face a ghost
sprung lightly from the sheets, a painless clock
that stops, quick as a thought, hands down.
But seven hours to drown! The taloned coast
grapples while the black surf dives, the fast rock
flashes as the last breath flies into stone.

The Visit

Knocking wood
to make her hearing aid work,
she asks in a tired thin voice
how long I'll be staying.

I've been praising New York,
green Liberty meeting ships,
the bay stealing up
to the ferryboat deck.

"So soon?" she says,
eyes focusing short
of where I sit. She holds
her cheek as if her tooth ached.

Getting up, she stoops
to pat the tabletop,
as if to verify by touch
what she's slowly losing sight of.

I don't know what I'd do
if her eyes lit up
when I entered a room,
if she touched my face

with affection. I take
her picture in the kitchen.
Her bobbed white hair
slants forward

on her cheek
as she bends over the sink
scrubbing by rote
her blue and white coffeepot

made of Corningware.
Only a daughter who loved her
could see a Vermeer woman
weighing gold.

*They shall take up serpents; and if they
drink any deadly thing it shall not hurt them.*
Mark 16:18

Wake of Brother Ray

All afternoon people file past, study him
like a text they're half afraid to memorize.
Some touch the single white glove hiding

the purple on his wrist where the timber
rattler struck. Some weep like the sisters
of Lazarus: the Lord too late. Sister

Betty, his widow, greets stranger or friend
with the same bearing-up smile. Come Sunday,
she will drive the hundred and fifty miles

from Galax to handle a snake religiously,
a crime in every state but West Virginia.
Their son, just twelve, pokes a note

in Ray's shirt pocket. She wonders what
he wrote, if he asked his father why. Ray,
bitten twice before, was healed both times

by faith alone. He wore a cap inscribed:
"God Said It, I Believe It, and That's It."
Last night she dreamed her husband's heel

slipped from her grasp. He fell until she woke
in the wide double bed, her nightgown soaked,
the sheets twisted into snakes.

Widower

Watching the young robins in the pear tree
learn to fly
I think of my wife

clinging to her limb.
In the darkness, I relish my grief.
It is safer to savor the dust she left

than sweep it away.
My trousers loosen.
To neighbors who bring me food

I curse my children.
I don't answer the phone.
I water her plants in the dining room,

secretly hoping
they too will die.
Today the African violets bloomed.

The Black Madonna

"You're interested in *me*," she says,
jabbing thumb to chest. My legs
twitch, threaten to buckle
as if I were watching my house
swim into flame. She is black as
Our Lady of Czestochowa, old
as Mary taking leave of earth
at Ephesus. Hand to hip, impatient,
she taps her foot. She is waiting
for me to see the woods.

This madonna carries no baby, wears
no veil. In the crook of her arm
sways a cracked leather purse
hefty as a club. The print
of her dress bristles with bearded
irises, and her eyes, fierce and bloodshot,
dart and dagger--as if she's had no sleep
in days, or maybe she drinks.

I hold my ears,
but her voice burning through my hands
is a torch lighting up
the place of the skull.

She's telling the trees
everything: how I cling to what's in front of me
and keep missing the point,
like Francis when he hears a voice
Rebuild my church
carting all those stones.

The sun ascends over her shoulder
while she pretends to disappear.
I take my first gulp of wildflower air.
I am shaking like Jesus in the garden,
quivering to be passed over.

For Rosemary

Midway through the night
you threw off the cape
of your body,

entered the labyrinth.
We'd looked for signs
you could hear us, held

as proof one blink
of an eyelid, poignant
as a father's ring

a friend wears
on his smallest finger,
the band too frail

to be sized. Worn and thin,
elegant to the end
as the filmy caftan

you wore to your last
dinner party, you
were like a cloud

casting its shadow
on a mountain stream,
running off without us.

Serbian

The dust raised by horses
settles on windows
streaked with blood,

on the bronze general
squarely stuck to his sword.
The silent bell

rusts in the steeple, exposed
and abandoned
to the will of God. The sky

hangs like a shroud
over ditches
filled with sons,

their eyes huge
with sorrow
lying open to the birds

whose song must end,
stifled
as they land on pale brows.

To a Daughter-in-Law

I think of infants carried to term, un-
wanted, their Moms' plots foiled—a willful fall
or tonics swallowed bringing on the spill
of bright red blood that says they've won.
They "go through with it," "have it," led by shame
or faith or guilt to walk the crooked mile
and bring a child to light, to the turnstile
without a coin. Spotting, at sea, you came
to me as Advent hurried toward the feast.
I reassured from books, my mother voice
a pair of hands to tuck you in, the least
sparrow in my mind flying blind, the choice
still ours to see in loss the hand of God
or sheer chance, the overbearing wild card.

Out-patients

In Alice blue gowns with three sleeves
we are some line-up.
Our smiles are far from sweet
and quick to die.
Eyes meet above old magazines:
something is not right
in paradise.

Vertical or prone,
we turn as we are told
by mole technicians used to the dark.
We bare flesh
convinced there is no innocence
in these machines
that tell what we have done
in secret.

Our cells are gypsies
twisting to some new and strange
choreography
toward an empty place
where violins fill
with water.

We push back death
like a cowlick
hoping it will hold
for the time being.

Elisabeth Murawski received the 2010 May Swenson Poetry Award for her collection *Zorba's Daughter*, which will be published by the Utah State University Press. She is the author of *Moon and Mercury* and a chapbook, *Troubled by an Angel*. Her poetry has appeared in *The Yale Review, The New Republic, Virginia Quarterly Review, The Ontario Review, The Literary Review, Field, Chelsea, Southern Review, Margie,* and others. Her poem "Abu Ghraib Suggests the Isenheim Altarpiece" won the 2006 Ann Stanford Prize. She was awarded a Hawthornden Fellowship in 2008. She resides in Alexandria, VA.

www.ingramcontent.com/pod-product-compliance
Lightning Source LLC
Chambersburg PA
CBHW031436040426
42444CB00006B/844